The Nature Kid's Guide to

IGUANAS

DAVID ANDERSON

For information address LP Media Inc. Publishing,
30012 Variolite St NW, Princeton MN 55371
www.lpmedia.org

Publication Data

Iguanas
The Nature Kid's Guide to Iguanas — First edition.

Summary: "Learn all about Iguanas, the Nature Kid Way"
— Provided by publisher.

ISBN: 979-8-89818-233-5

[1. Iguanas – Non-Fiction] I. Title.

Title: The Nature Kid's Guide to Iguanas

CONTENTS

TROPICAL TURF

Rustle! A green iguana crawls along a warm branch.

High in the treetops of a steaming tropical rainforest, a large green lizard sits perfectly still in the sun. This is an iguana, and this warm, leafy world is exactly where it belongs.

Iguanas are built for the **tropics**. They need heat from the sun to move, hunt, and digest their food. Without it, their bodies simply shut down.

Most iguanas spend their days resting on branches near rivers, soaking up warmth and watching the world below. The hotter and greener the habitat, the happier the iguana.

ISLAND IGUANAS

Marine iguanas sneeze out extra salt through special glands in their nose — it looks like they're spitting!

Splash! A marine iguana dives off into the water.

Iguanas live across a huge part of the world. Green iguanas are found from Mexico through Central America and into South America. They also live on many Caribbean islands.

Marine iguanas live only on the Galápagos Islands. These dark lizards dive into the cold ocean to eat algae — the only lizard on Earth that feeds in the sea.

Other kinds live in very different places. The rhinoceros iguana lives on rocky Caribbean islands. The desert iguana survives the blazing heat of the American Southwest. Same family, very different worlds.

SIZE UP

The biggest green iguanas can stretch longer than a bicycle from nose to tail tip!

Thud! A big iguana lands on the forest floor with a bump.

Green iguanas are big lizards. Really big. They can grow over five feet long — about as tall as a grown-up! Most of that length is tail. The tail stretches longer than the rest of the body combined. A big green iguana can weigh up to eleven pounds.

The rhinoceros iguana is shorter but much stockier. It grows to about four feet and is built more like a small tank than a tree climber.

Desert iguanas are much smaller. They only grow to about sixteen inches — small enough to fit in your backpack!

SCALY STYLE

Scritch! An iguana scratches its rough, bumpy skin on bark.

Iguanas are covered in tough **scales**. These scales protect them like tiny shields. Some are small and smooth. Others are large and bumpy.

Rhinoceros iguanas have bumps on their nose that look like little horns. These bumps make this iguana easy to spot in a crowd.

All iguanas have sharp claws and strong legs. A flap of skin hangs under their chin called a dewlap. Males have bigger dewlaps than females.

Iguanas shed their old skin in pieces as they grow — it can take weeks to peel off completely!

SUPER SENSES

FUN FACT!

An iguana's third eye is covered by a pale scale — look closely at the top of their head!

Flick! An iguana's tongue tastes the air for clues.

Iguanas have amazing senses. They can see colors that people cannot see, including ultraviolet light. Their sharp eyes help them spot food and danger from far away.

Green iguanas have a special trick. A tiny spot on top of their head senses light. It is called a third eye, but it cannot see pictures. It just tells them if a shadow passes overhead.

Iguanas also use their tongue to smell. They flick it out to taste the air. This helps them learn what is around them.

SPIKY SHIELDS

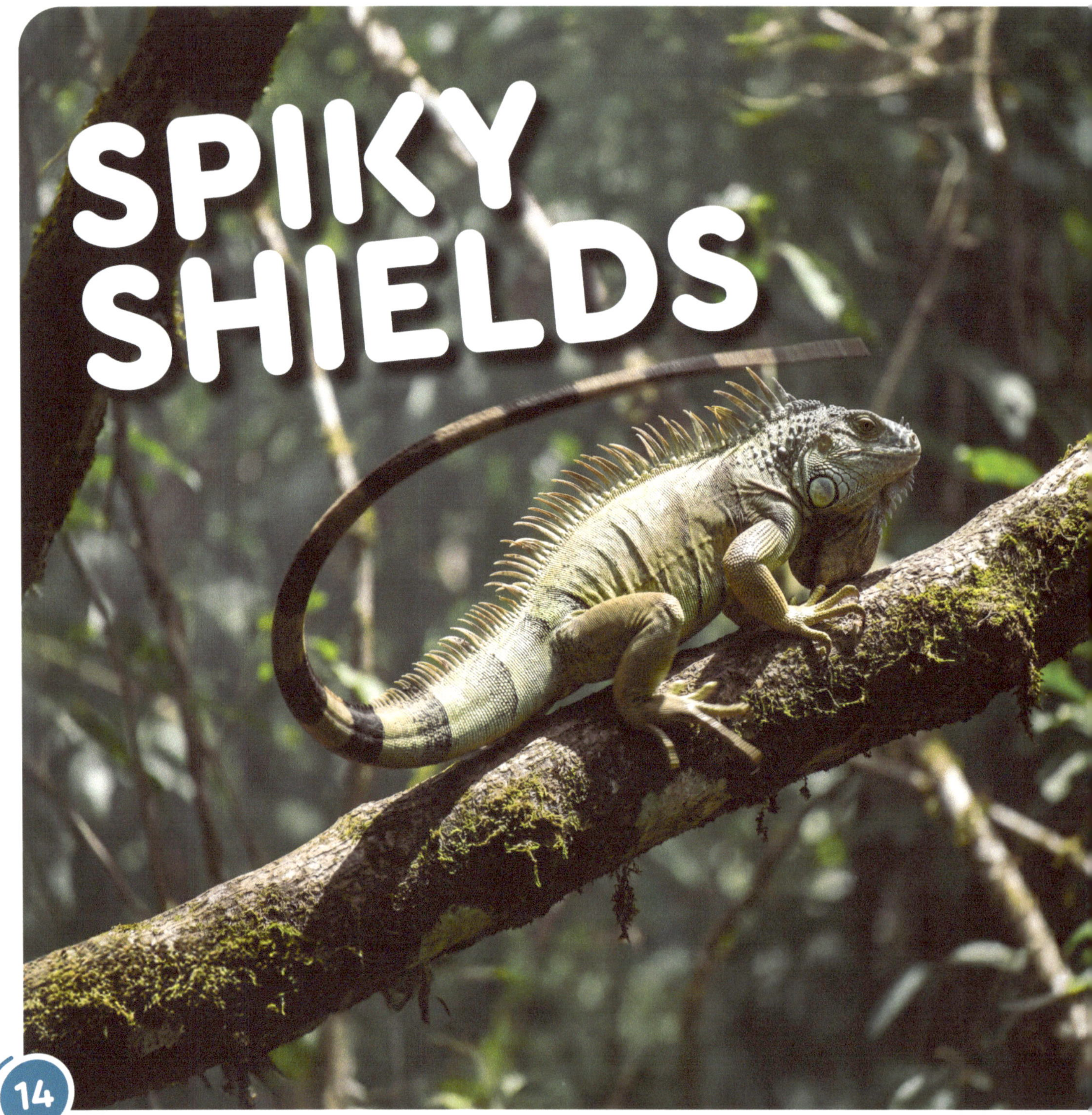

Whap! An iguana whips its long tail at a sneaky snake.

Iguanas have many ways to stay safe. Sharp spines run down their back like a row of tiny swords. These spines make them hard to swallow.

An iguana's tail is a strong weapon. One swing hits like a whip. The smack is hard enough to sting and leave a mark!

Iguanas can also bite if they must. Their jaws are strong and full of small teeth. But most iguanas try to run away first.

An iguana can break off its tail to escape a predator — and grow a new one over several months!

LEAFY LUNCH
DID YOU KNOW?
Green iguanas have special bacteria in their gut that help them digest tough leaves.
16

Crunch! An iguana rips a big green leaf with its teeth.

Most iguanas love to eat plants. Green iguanas munch on leaves, flowers, and fruit. They spend hours each day chewing their leafy meals.

Young iguanas sometimes eat bugs too. The extra protein helps them grow big and fast. But older iguanas stick mostly to greens.

Marine iguanas eat a special sea plant called **algae**. They dive underwater and scrape it off wet rocks with their teeth. Each kind of iguana has its own favorite food.

HEAD BOBS

Bob, bob, bob! An iguana pumps its head up and down.

Iguanas talk without making a sound. They use body moves to send messages. Other iguanas know just what each move means.

A slow head bob means hello or all clear. A fast head bob? That is a warning. It tells others to stay away right now.

Iguanas also puff out their **dewlap**. The colorful chin flap gets attention fast. It helps iguanas talk to each other from far away.

Each iguana bobs its head in its own special pattern — scientists can tell individuals apart just by watching!

HUNGRY
HUNTERS

Screech! A hawk swoops down toward a resting iguana.

Many animals hunt iguanas. Hawks swoop down from the sky with sharp talons. Snakes slither up trees to catch them while they sleep.

On the ground, foxes and cats are a danger. Wild dogs hunt iguanas on some islands. Even big fish can grab iguanas near water.

Baby iguanas face the most risk. They are small and easy to catch. Staying hidden is their best hope for survival.

On the Galapagos Islands, large Sally Lightfoot crabs hunt and eat baby iguanas right on the beach!

QUICK ESCAPE

An iguana can hold its breath underwater for up to 30 minutes — that's as long as some seals!

Whoosh! An iguana leaps from a high branch into the river.

When danger is near, iguanas act fast. Green iguanas often jump from trees into water below. They can fall over 40 feet and land safely!

Once in the water, iguanas swim like champions. They tuck their legs tight and swing their powerful tail. The water carries them far from danger in seconds.

Some iguanas stay very still instead. Their green or brown color blends in with the trees. **Predators** walk right past without seeing them.

CLIMB HIGH

Iguanas have five toes on each foot, and each toe has a curved claw perfect for gripping bark!

Zip! An iguana scurries straight up a tall tree trunk.

Iguanas are born to climb. Their toes grip bark like tiny hooks. They can race up a tree in seconds flat.

Up in the branches, balance matters most. Their long tail acts like a tightrope walker's pole. It keeps them steady on even the thinnest branches.

On the ground, iguanas can move fast too. They rise up on their back legs and run. Some can dash nearly 21 miles per hour — faster than most kids can sprint!

SUN SOAKERS

Iguanas sometimes bask in groups and pile on top of each other — the ones on bottom get squished but stay extra warm!

Plop! A desert iguana flops onto a warm, flat rock to bask.

Iguanas start each day in the warm sun. They lie on rocks or branches to soak up heat. This warms their bodies so they can get going.

Desert iguanas love heat more than most. They stay active even when temperatures hit 115 degrees! Other lizards hide, but desert iguanas keep going strong.

As the sun goes down, iguanas find a safe spot. They rest on branches or in rock cracks. A good night's sleep keeps them ready for the next day.

LONER LIZARDS

Hiss! A Galapagos land iguana warns another to find its own rock.

Most iguanas like to be alone. They do not live in big groups or families. Each iguana picks its own space to live.

The biggest males claim the best spots. They sit on the highest rocks or sunniest patches. Smaller iguanas must find a spot farther away or risk a fight.

Sometimes iguanas do gather close. They may share a sunny area or a good food spot. But even then, they keep a careful eye on each other.

FLASHY FLIRTS

Male marine iguanas turn bright red and green during mating season — the most colorful males attract the most females!

Puff! A male iguana blows up his bright dewlap to show off.

At mating time, male iguanas show off. They turn bright colors and strut around like tiny dinosaurs. Each male tries hard to get noticed.

Males sometimes fight over a female. They push and shove with their bodies. The stronger male usually wins, and the loser walks away.

The female watches and picks the best male. She wants the one that looks biggest and strongest. Then they pair up for the season.

TINY TOTS
DID YOU KNOW?
A baby iguana has a special egg tooth just for breaking open its shell — it falls off a few days after hatching!

Crack! A tiny iguana pokes its nose out of a white egg.

Mother iguanas dig a deep hole to lay their eggs. Each one may lay 20 to 70 eggs at once! The eggs sit in warm dirt for about two months.

When the babies hatch, they dig out together. Baby iguanas are bright green and very small — only about 6 inches long from nose to tail.

Right away, the little ones must find food. They eat tiny leaves and bits of flowers. Growing up fast is the key to staying safe from predators.

SOLO START

DID YOU KNOW?
Baby iguanas often follow older iguanas to learn where to find the best food — like having a big brother show you around!

Poof! The mother iguana slips away and leaves the nest.

Once a mother iguana lays her eggs, she is done. She covers the nest with dirt and walks away. The babies must make it on their own from day one.

Baby iguanas stick together at first. A group of brothers and sisters is safer than one alone. They help each other watch for danger.

As they grow, young iguanas go their own way. They learn to find food and shelter alone. Being on their own makes them strong and independent.

ANCIENT ARMOR

Iguana relatives have been around for over 200 million years — they lived alongside the dinosaurs!

Stomp! A rhinoceros iguana marches across sun-warmed stone.

Iguanas have been around for millions of years. They have many tricks that help them last. Tough skin, strong legs, and sharp senses keep them alive generation after generation.

Some iguanas face new dangers today. Cars, cats, and lost habitat are big problems. People are working hard to keep wild iguanas safe.

Rhinoceros iguanas live on just a few Caribbean islands. Animal helpers watch over them with care. Every healthy iguana matters for the future of the species.

SPOT ONE

FUN
FACT!
Wild iguanas can live for over
20 years — some scientists
have tracked the same iguanas
for decades!

Creak! An iguana suns itself high up on a branch.

Want to see a wild iguana? In the United States, green iguanas live in southern Florida. If you visit, look near warm rivers and sunny trees where iguanas rest on branches soaking up the morning sun.

Not close to Florida? Many zoos across the country keep iguanas, including marine iguanas and rhinoceros iguanas. Ask a keeper about feeding time for the best view.

Be quiet and move slowly wherever you watch them. Iguanas scare easily — the best nature watchers always leave animals in peace.

GLOSSARY

tropics

Warm areas near the
middle of the Earth

scales

Small, flat plates that
cover a reptile's body

dewlap

A flap of skin under a
lizard's chin

algae

Tiny green plants that
grow in water or on rocks

predators

Animals that hunt and eat
other animals